2nd Edition

THE MAGIC OF BUSINESS AND SALE IN MULTI-NETWORK

Made by
Juan Carlos Martín

www.juancarlosmartin.info
info@juancarlosmartin.info
April 2019

Note to readers: This book is more a theoretical than practical manual, my experience includes several years in the online business success ...
"The Magic of MLM and Network Business Sale"

Carlos Martín @Juan April 2019
Desktop publishing: Juan Carlos Martín
www.juancarlosmartin.info
info@juancarlosmartin.info
Graphic design: Francisco Torreblanca Peralta
www.franperalta.com
Printed in Spain

READER'S NOTE

Juan Carlos Martín He is a born entrepreneur. After several years in traditional business, he began researching the internet and discovered a whole world of possibilities.

Today it is developing a successful business networking, author of the books "The Magic of Facebook" and "The Magic of Internet Business". Creator of the Online Academy www.lamagiadelosnegociosporinternet.es and the **Online program Magic Internet**

He is founder of Digital Marketing Agency JCM.

His great passion, help others as Online Marketing Consultant and Advisor Digital Tools.

DEDICATION

My soul mates and my life, my wife Sonia and my sons Adrian and Saul; for your continued support, for your unconditional love, for never having tried to cut the wings, by value me as I am, listening my words and silences, for being my support and support for electing me to share life and for your generosity in allowing me pawning much time and energy on other tasks. I love you.

My soul brother José Luis Martín-Muñoz Macho, sadly died on April 28, 2013, for all the support she offered. I know I have greatly enjoyed seeing the publication of this book.

THANKS

I dedicate these lines to my students, each and every one of Exialoe independent distributors, who trusted me as their leader; each person and friend with whom I shared scenarios, revealing another lifestyle; mentors and partners who have, from all angles, to be a successful person in my business.

THANK YOU

INDEX

MODULE 1
BUSINESS MODEL

1. For whom is this business model.
2. My personal experience
3. Differences Between Network Marketing and traditional business.
4. Legal information
5. Distinguishing Multilevel system (MLM) and a system Pyramidal
6. Network Marketing we do every day
7. Network Marketing you will do from now

MODULE 2 :
OPERATION OF THIS BUSINESS MODEL

1. A little history about Network Marketing
2. Passive income
3. The Money Flow Quadrant
4. Choose the right MLM company
5. Products or services sold
6. Training and working tools
7. Generate income with this system
8. Become a leader in MLM
9. The day to day of a Networker

MODULE 3
All the secrets of this business model

1. MLM breaks all the established schemes
2. Offering a MLM
3. What usually fail in MLM
4. How to Succeed in MLM
5. Your business!
6. Knowledge about the product or service
7. Knowledge of the Company and the business system
8. theoretical and implementation
9. A great motivation and self confidence
10. Time management
11. Daily work plan
12. Visualize the goal
13. Online school
14. Products or services
15. Arguments of products or services
16. Arguments of this business system
17. I give you some ideas
18. Ways to offer business
19. goals
20. Training.

MODULE 4
Tips that will lead to success in network marketing

1. The importance of choosing a company and a good Mentor
2. It depends only on you
3. Define your goals and your dreams
4. Excuses for not starting a business
5. mentality Multilevel
6. Define your identity
7. As offering your company as project or as an opportunity
8. Here are some ideas for direct sales of products of Health and Welfare
9. 10 Tips to invite a Network Marketing Business
10. In this you had not thought
11. Multilevel sell products to friends
12. If you only looking for money you will not be happy
13. How to get support from your family
14. Attention!! beware dreamthieves, not to steal your freedom
15. 10 keys to detect toxic people

-FOREWORD-

Magic Juan Carlos Martin ... José Campos Martin

It is curious that life sometimes gives you a few things that you least expect, and gifts that are priceless and that was for me to have met Juan Carlos.

From a very young man I looked about 19 years ando business of all kinds, physicists at the beginning and online today. And looking and looking teach me a free lecture by a certain Daniel Garcia Calvo in my city. Curious about everything, I ask my work hours cooking teacher, to attend the talk. I did not know the gift I would give my life a few months later ...

After seeing the conference; Several months later, I stand a course taught by Dani a day, a Sunday. I sit there in front as I can and see a person with crossed in front, behind glasses with a wonderful smile arms. Black dress offers me an advertisement for something I was wandering looking for someone to guide me to the truth. Because for me the truth is what works, what you have results, that to me is the truth. And Juan Carlos had them ... From that moment I got on her hands and kept calling to help me for what later became my work, a private collection of cookbook, soccer and humor, with more than 40 titles. An automated business that my "Helmano" as I call it affectionately, as barbarians activated with these business skills online.

And as you know this is yours also part ...

Currently I have the pleasure to develop more than three businesses online and networkers with Juan Carlos and the truth I strongly urge you not let pass the opportunity to acquire this masterpiece that only Juan Carlos can put in your hands.

And the truth, as I said, is what works; and he knows like nobody else, do it.

Jose Campos Martin
Restaurateur Chef, lecturer, writer and entrepreneur On-line.
www.josecamposmartin.com

INTRODUCTION

This book is entirely practical and has been entirely developed by Juan Carlos Martín Muñoz-Macho, much collecting data from some of the most important Networkers and other big part of my training and experience.

This book, it aims to teach in depth this business system.

A business system for the future, but above all this, since it is implanted in the best companies worldwide and increasingly Spanish companies use.

In the first module, you will get started in the world of Network Marketing and you'll learn how it works and how to differentiate it from other business models.

In the second module, you'll know more about this business system, how it works internally and how you can make money in a company that works with this system.

In the third module, I will explain the practical part, what I mean by this? I will dedicate it to explain important concepts, you should consider if you work with this system business or want to start doing it.

In the fourth module I'll give you some tips that will make you reach the success or you stay in the same place so far, remember this phrase, "to have different results, you have to do different things," you want to be one of the bunch or you want to stand out from your competition as a leader or mentor in your company.

I have to tell you, if you're looking for or what you expect of Network Marketing or MLM is a way to earn money effortlessly and immediately, you're in the wrong book.

This is not a "book" of those who promise that you'll make money from home without moving and working 1 hour a day, which I offer in this book is to have knowledge of this business model.

There are many types and business models. Some of you already know, such as traditional business models, such as small and medium businesses or franchises, but what really sets this type of business of others, what you learn in this book.

Read and find out.

Business system that will try in this book has nothing to do with what you know so far, it's more, I dare say that is totally opposite.

TRADITIONAL COMPANY AND FRANCHISE

TRADITIONAL COMPANY

- Great risk
- Local investment
- Vehicles
- Tools
- Machinery
- Employees?
- Gender investment
- Rent, electricity and water
- Stress
- Little free time
- Retirement?

AND FRANCHISE

MORE:
- Entry fees and fees
- Fixed term contract

In my opinion, this type of business, is a business model almost perfect. A system that you can dedicate yourself professionally and with which you can get to earn an income in constant growth and stability, which today can not be achieved with a traditional job.

This business model will also help to achieve something very important today, improve your quality of life.

As I promised in the first part, I will explain and introduce the "Network Marketing", a business model for the present and future. Of course, as in any business, you have to strive to achieve all your goals, but that work will be rewarded.

You are ready? Well, let's begin.

MODULE 1
BUSINESS MODEL

1. Who is this business model.

The first thing I have to say is that this business model is not for everyone. Being so, if you feel identified with some of the features below detallarte will not waste time. I appreciate enormously interested sorry, but realistically, you will not get anything with this business model.

This business model is not for what I call "analysts". For me, analysts are those who do not stop searching and studying business or business systems, but that never finish developing one. If you want, it is to expand knowledge and nothing else, better buy a book of business management.

You learn a lot, sure, but not teach you to put a going concern with a system that really works.

Nor is it for people who believe there is a system or a business model that will make you money without any effort or investment, either time or money.

Any company or any business you want to start, either with this model or other system, will require an investment in more or less time and money; the difference is that in this type of business model, emplearás further time and less money.

You'll have to invest time in your training, know the products or services that will work. Learn all that entails MLM takes time and dedication.

Nor it is for anyone who thinks it will start making money by magic, the overnight, I'm sorry, but I have to tell you that this will not happen.

If you do not like studying, working on new things every day, innovate and ultimately be continually open to all developments as they emerge, if this is not, this business is not for you.

If you are one of those people that when he takes action and does not work out does not seek its own failures, but all he seeks is who he is because of his failure because you think you have been cheated by not getting the final results, neither is for you. This business model requires effort and sacrifice.

If you are a person, who does not like to make decisions and act for itself immediately when the opportunity arises, this business is not for you.
And finally, and possibly one of the most important things is that if you do not believe in yourself, do not think you can get everything you propose, however hard it may be, can never professionally devote to this type of business.

For the years of business experience I have in this business model and how many entrepreneurs I've met, those who actually have managed to reach their goals are those who did not meet any of the above features; so if you feel identified with any of the characteristics described above, do not continue reading this book.

Now this book and this business model is for you if ...:
- You are a person who likes to learn new ways of doing business, open-minded.
- If you believe that the best investment of your time and your money is in your personal training.
- If you are a responsible and consistent with their actions.
- If you do not want anything or anyone control your life or your time or your money.
- If you do not want bosses.
- If you have within you an active leader who starts immediately when you see a business opportunity.
- And above all, if you want to change your life, give a 360 and get down to work to achieve the financial freedom that you need both.

Then this book does is for you.

Still here? I like that. You mean you really are a person who will take this book and that it will carry out positive action in their lives.

2. My personal experience

As I said before, my name is Juan Carlos Martin and then want to tell you something about my life, so you can know me better and know who the author of this work and why I did it.

When I decided to write this book?
When my friend Jose Campos began to cheer and to insist share my knowledge and experience with anyone that might need that to date shared individually and privately with my fellow network.

Having worked for years as a hotelier entrepreneur, I have a Digital Marketing Agency Online, Online Marketing Consultant and Advisor Digital Tools for companies and entrepreneurs.

I dedicate a small portion of my time to online training for a team of Independent Distributors a MLM business, have a sales network of more than 500 people.

Everything is online, or almost everything, so I work from my office at home, which would be the dream of many.

For many who they do not have never done, commenting that having an online business and work from home, means the number of hours you work each day is 50% more than if you had a job with a fixed schedule and away from home.

In my professional experience, I can also describe how a traditional business or franchise works; since I have been fortunate to work both systems, here I I will highlight the highlights of these two activities.

And I say "lucky" because it has made me appreciate much more this system business, we will try throughout this book.

3. Differences between Network Marketing and traditional business.

Network Marketing is a business system that a company uses to sell and distribute their products or services, by creating networks of distributors and consumers without having to go through intermediaries.

With this system, as with any other, the company intends to sell more products reach more end users and expand the company.

What we avoid with this system is that the product or service unnecessary passes hands, that all they would be making the final product or service. With this image you will see it more clearly.

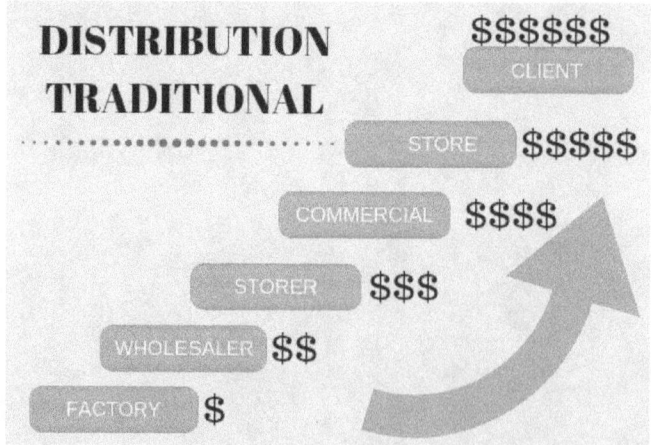

Which supports you with these companies or factories, it is that they can not sell the product directly to customers, they have no shop and serve customers. Always sale must go through an authorized distributor, ie us.

These companies make, since all these steps are saved and traditional business as a result can offer a better price the product or service and we as distributors earn commissions by the company offer us to save costs.

Then you call the factory and tell them you want to be a distributor?

Here it is also big in this business; they'll tell you to be a distributor must come referred by another distributor, because as says the word "Network" is what networking is.

What I want to say with this is that just for the simple fact that dealer a Network Marketing company, and have great benefits because:

- You can buy products that other people can not.
- You're going to buy a discount, who otherwise would not have.
- You also have the ability to sell and profit from them.
- But you can also take people to the company's distributors who want to be like you and make money so they sell.

You can also collect revenue every time those associated clients you buy, what are called residual income from those discussed in depth later.

It is one of the most important features that differentiates a traditional MLM business system.

So multilevel marketing works. Simple right?

It is very important to know that this has nothing to do with a pyramid scheme.

4. Legal Information

The fundamental thing you should know is that pyramid schemes are prohibited.

Network Marketing is totally legal and is included in the "Planning Law 7/1996 and 26/1991 Retail".

Also, in Network Marketing no matter where in the network situation you are, if you work more than someone who has come before you to the company, he will get more benefits.

In a pyramid scheme that is not possible, which is positioned above Magaña and the one below is the least wins, no matter what endeavor and work.

5. Differences between a multilevel system (MLM) and a system Pyramidal

It is important that at no time confused and think that MLM is a pyramid scheme, because they have nothing to do.

It is a very grave mistake that many people to compare them or even say it's the same.

Not so, keep that very clear.

To give even become clearer and see the difference, if you offer a business and you're not sure if MLM or pyramid here's an image that reflects the differences:

MULTILEVEL	PIRAMIDAL
- - Small entrance fee	- High income fee
- Quality Products	- Products of dubious quality
- Purpose to sell	- Objective to recruit
- Return guarantee	- No warranty
- A long-term business	-Get rich in a short time
- Recognition of effort	- Effort means nothing
- Reduced or no stock	- You have to accumulate product
- Freedom	- Pressure
- Legal	- Illegal

6. Network Marketing we do every day

Network Marketing system is used by very large and very prestigious companies and have been doing since the 50s.

By this I tell you, nobody is inventing anything here, but everything is invented, tested and fully validated by thousands of people.

This system has a very simple operation.

It is so simple that you do each day without realizing it. Yes, yes, it is.

I'll give you an example and see how fast you can understand it and you'll see as you perform every day without knowing it and of course without winning anything.

Until now.

The worst thing is not that the worst thing is that every day we make dozens of recommendations of products and services that have been satisfied and received absolutely nothing in return. No money, no discounts or special offers.

For this reason, some employers thought Why can we not do something to reward everyone who recommend us and we can all stand to gain?

NETWORK MARKETING WHAT YOU DO EVERYDAY WITHOUT ACKNOWLEDGING

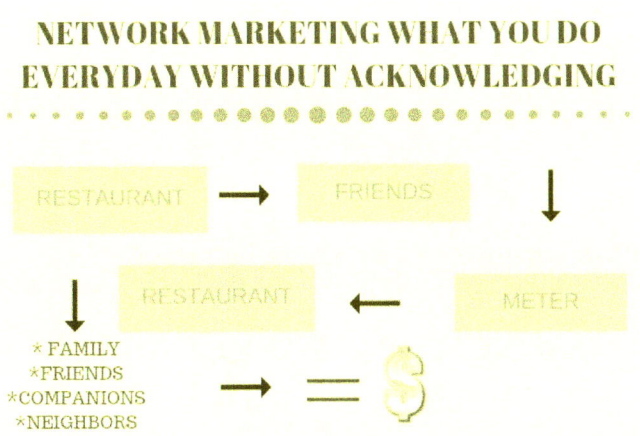

7. Network Marketing you will do from now

And the question asked in the previous point and a research by the pioneers, was born on Network Marketing, Network Marketing or MLM.

Now and forever, with this type of business, every time you suggest and to recommend products to you so good results have given you or you liked, you'll make money.

What's more, notes the following image:

As noted in the previous picture, let's imagine that where it says "you" is the person who recommends a product or service (in this case you); This person would recommend the product or service to

Manuel, Amparo, Peter, John, Martha, Luis and Paco; this would be your first generation.

But now there is more, it recommended Amparo turn to Miguel and Alfredo; and it recommends Pedro Alberto, Diego and Jose; Luis and it also recommends that Eva and Ana, this would be your second generation.

But now it recommended Alberto Andrew; Joseph recommended Carlos and Teresa; and it recommends Eva Marta, this would be your third generation and so on to levels that allows you to the Company. And as your network grows you will be receiving commissions from the sales of your referrals and sales of your recommended recommended.

How about? Great right? As this is not all this money will come to you without having to do anything else.

You have worked hard and have brought your products and business to many people. This system rewards you for it.

And so we can follow up several lines down and many friends as you want on each line. I think it's fairly simple example and generally explains how the Network Marketing.

This is just an example, so you can understand the system that follows. There is no limit to friends, ie, there is no earnings limit.

Now you get for recommending products to you go well and can help many people. In addition've helped friends to generate income I extras.Lo most important is that these gains the cobrarás month and forever.

It is the way the Network Marketing rewards those who work.

And here, the first module of the book "The Magic of Business and Sale in Red".

Did you like it? Would you like to continue and keep learning?

Then we continue with the second module and you can get much more information and more details on this business system with which you can make a living.

MODULE 2
HOW DOES THIS BUSINESS MODEL

1. A bit of history about the Network Marketing

In this second module, let's go a little more in this business system, the Network Marketing.

I'll give you something more advanced information, so you can know in depth how to be a professional Networker.

It all started in the 40s and 50s, when an American company realized that many of the vendors who came to work at the company and many of the guests were friends, acquaintances and relatives of vendors and customers who already had the company.

In this way, they thought it would be interesting if everyone consumed and sold a small amount of their products, increase sales volume much more than a few of the best sellers they could hire.

So combining these two concepts, they began to create the first form of Network Marketing. All customers and distributors had an equal right to distribute products of the company and benefited by recommending and selling those products, with payment of fees. So the company began to grow exponentially.

With this system, anyone could make money selling and recommending products, but it really was very high profits was to form your own network of consumers and recommend products company.

Formerly, in many cases, to develop a business Multilevel a large volume of sales and consumption were required, so that was not available to everyone. But today, the demands have changed, to the point that anyone can start their own business with this system.

If to this, we add new technologies that exist today and everyone has available (internet, mobile phone, social networks), this business system becomes the best way to have your own business, if your own boss without spending the amounts of money than a conventional business requires without taking unnecessary risks.

Formerly, to reach the same number of people who can access which now still sitting at the computer, it took months.

Today with social networks, mobile phones and other technologies, you can reach hundreds and thousands of people in a month without even leaving home.

Furthermore, if we add that today, the number of people with whom we interact on a daily basis has increased dramatically, we have a capacity to expand in this huge business.
This does not mean that we should not trabajárselo, not at all, but investing half hours or less you spend your conventional job mid-term results will be very good.

Multilevel Marketing system, have implemented many large companies, to create the largest possible expansion, companies like IBM or Amazon.

At its inception this system had many critics, because as I said before, did not know differentiate a (illegal) pyramid scheme because it believed that the benefits obtained from this system arose exclusively by incorporating new distributors to the network. And this is what really sets a pyramid scheme of Multilevel Marketing.

So, if you ever come across any company in which the main source of income that you generate is to incorporate new distributors to your network, distrusts totally, because that company will almost certainly, a pyramid scheme.

Now a little theory What is passive income?

2. Passive Income

To answer this question, I have to mention before Toru Kiyosaki Robert. If you have researched a little about Network Marketing sure you've heard of it and if not, I will teach you something about it, because what I will try in this section was spread by this author in his books.

Robert Toru Kiyosaki, born on April 8, 1947, in Hilo, Hawaii. He is an entrepreneur, investor, writer, speaker and American motivational speaker. He has written 15 books, of which some of them have become number one in the lists of major sales in the United States.

I highly recommend you read everything you can about it, because it will serve you much help recommend.

This gentleman has spread and continues to spread wherever he goes the concept of "Passive Income" and defines it broadly as:

"Income we receive for jobs that do not require our presence "
Such as rents, dividends from investments, interest, etc.

This is important, because as Robert Toru Kiyosaki says "have taught us to work for money, but do not know how to make money work for us."

To help you understand this perfectly, we will use the "Cashflow Quadrant" Robert Toru Kiyosaki who created it and explains it very well.

3. Money Flow Quadrant

Robert Toru Kiyosaki Mr. created this chart to explain his theory of "Cashflow Quadrant". So at first glance, you will pass like me when I saw it the first time, I knew absolutely nothing about what it meant, but once I explained I could understand and is an overwhelming logic.

Look at business owners (D), do not talk about business. The vast majority of entrepreneurs do not have a company that has a system that allows it to function without them.

To find out if you are an entrepreneur in the new economy, you just have to ask the question Robert Toru Kiyosaki suggests that Can you go on vacation 15 days in your business and that is absolutely not notice anything? Moreover, what continues to grow and generate more revenue?

Most entrepreneurs will answer this question no. The greatness of Network Marketing is exactly this.

If you have worked long enough and well enough, you'll be away from your business and it will not only generate income by itself, but also grow.

4. Choose the best MLM company

Generally, when you think introduce in Network Marketing, you will look for a company that provides you a salable product or service, high quality and repetitive use and everything you need to start and develop your business.

This we have just said is very important because when choosing what business to start forjarte as a professional Network Marketing, you have to consider all these things:

The first thing to do is a little research on the company that you have set to develop as a Networker.

You have to inquire about their history, the years of working with this system, testimonies of people who have worked on it, what countries can develop your business, sales in recent years, etc.

This information, right now is very easy to get on the internet, so do not cut and looking all the information needed to choose the best company.

Above all, seeks views of people who are in the business and make money.

Why do I say this? Chances are, you find opinions discontented people because you do not get the expected revenue because it has not expanded as they had assured him he would and others, but I assure you that 100% of these cases is a bad practice them themselves.

These businesses, these companies and these systems are not just invented, they spent more than 50 years in the market allowing renowned companies expand.

These systems are more than tested and always work and when you follow the guidelines people who have actually taken the expected income with these companies.

Before you decide to start working with a network marketing company, you should take a number of precautions. The points we will see, are those who have to alert you that the company is not good for you:

- If you promise big profits in a short time
- If you are forced to pay an entrance fee
- If you pay only for each person you bring to the company
- If you are forced to consume each month
- If you require a minimum sales per month
- If the products they sell are of dubious quality
- If the company has less than 10 years old
- If you have no training department

Do not think to start a business like this is easy. Any company has its complication potential and as a good businessman you are, 95% of things, both good and bad that occur in your new business will be thanks to you.

As I said above, both good and bad. And even if your sponsor will help you in everything you can and the company gives you the best tools on the market, everything will depend solely on you and your dedication.

5. products or services sold.

the type of product or service must also take into account that the company offers to distribute it. You must consider some aspects of the products or services to decantarte by a company or another:

- They must be of the highest quality
- They must be unique
- They must be indispensable for anyone
- Must be repetitive consumption
- They must be different from those of competitors
- They must be affordable
- Must meet deadlines
- Should ensure the existence of stock

6. Training and tools

One thing, for me more important that you must consider is the system and training tools that comprise the company or the team you join, to help you learn more about the product or service, technical sales, marketing tools, etc.

All this I consider extremely important, because if for example the company has a system Online or training physical, meetings or courses for your area regularly, the process of adaptation and learning will be much shorter and learn every day in these formations it will help you keep your motivation and your network.

You can train in much less time and start to get results much sooner. However, if the company in which you notice no such training and other tools, you probably desmotives, for slow learning and not get the desired results it is easy to give up on your efforts.

You should check that the company can bring you training in all these fields:
- General MLM training.
- Product training.
- Sales techniques training.
- Training in new technologies.
- Marketing tools.

This aspect is very important so do not neglect can be the difference between success and failure both in this business as in any.

7. Generate revenue with this system

If you have already opted for a company that meets your expectations and you followed my directions, you have probably chosen a company that take a long time to market, in which many people have tried their products, so it will be known as your system and surely generate millions of sales a year, it will be time to get to work actively; They choosing rather not have to make an effort to publicize the brand, and strive to demonstrate that the products are good and they work, because surely there are hundreds of studies and comparisons to demonstrate why their products are better or have better than the competition.

A clear example is "McDonalds". An entrepreneur opens a "McDonalds" and not have to worry about nothing but train and train all you can because people already know "McDonalds" people and would "McDonalds" before he bought the franchise.

Well, it's a graphic example, we can not compare economically, since riding a franchise of "McDonalds" takes an investment of 1 million euros.

It is good to know that in a few years that investment pay for themselves, but do you have that million euros? I do not.

With this example, I want to give you to understand is that almost all companies working with Network Marketing, need not worry or manufacturing, or distribution, or anything else that is not distributing the products and publicize new distributors business so good that you are doing.

In a conventional business, in most cases you should worry about more than 80% of those aspects. Needless to say, that to mount the first thing you need is an average investment of € 30,000 for office rent, deposit, insurance, contracts, salaries, investment in the stock ...

If you decide to dedicate yourself to Multilevel, all the above problems disappear.

There will be others of course, but problems will depend on you and only you can solve smoothly.

Well, if you have not had a traditional business desconocerás all these aspects, but you can get an idea and if you had know what I'm talking about.

8. become a leader in MLM

What separates success from failure on many occasions in any business and much more in MLM, it is know to be a true leader. And for that you must maintain a series of daily habits and attitudes that expose you below:

- Keep your day-to-day motivation
- Positive attitude
- Be competitive with yourself
- Be consistent with your equipment daily
- The objectives are to fulfill marques you
- Be humble and share
- You must have capacity for learning
- Stay permissive and tolerant
- Help your team and teach them everything you know

9. The daily life of a Networker

As in any business, we must follow some guidelines, some "rules" and steps.

This business model would not be outdone and that really success is assured must follow the steps I show below:

- You must ask yourself why you planning to do this kind of business
- Define your goals in the short, medium and long term
- Draw a plan of action to reach them
- Commit to your goals
- Believe in what you do
- Asociate with enthusiastic people like you
- Use all the tools that help you to publicize your business

We have already completed two modules of the book "The Magic of MLM and Network Business Sale" of Network Marketing.

But now comes the most important, although I've shown you so far is not less.

In the third module, I'll show data particularly relevant, since I will provide strategies and concepts that I have done to succeed if or if.

We will delve into practice, so far I have taught some theory, but from now you must put into practice what they have learned and take action.

I also wanted to thank you personally for having come this far. You have done a good job, but now you have left most importantly, get going.

Nothing will have served these two read if you do not really pay attention to this third part of the book and do not put into action starting today to start creating your own business parties.

MODULE 3
All the secrets of this business model

1. MLM breaks all the established schemes

- It's a nice job and where you feel valued / ay rewarded / a
- It is a business where everyone has the same opportunities, regardless of age (+18 years), sex, religion, race, etc.
- You depend solely on you, your effort and your team
- You do not need a college degree, rather cultivate human qualities
- It is a business system that works even in the height of crisis
- You will help other people to earn income and improve their quality of life
- Daily income
- Income increase every month
- Security, tranquility and a comfortable retirement
- Impressive quality of life
- Owning your time
- A legacy for your family. Every effort you make will be a legacy for them in the future
- You have better health to enjoy life

As an Independent Distributor you are or if you are considering the possibility to be, you have to know that if you do your job well and if you're persistent, I can assure you that in 1, 2 or 3 years you'll be earning more than many of the jobs that exist today and satisfaction of owning / a of your time.

There are people who make it earlier and others a little later, but all who remain come to get it.

In any case, you may decide not to devote to this business 100%, because maybe you just want to get some extra income. This is fine, however, will see that with a few hours of painstaking work and dedication a week, your income month will increase to month and consolidated, which will make you ask yourself the dedicate exclusively or not this type of business.

I want you to know and enjoy the true potential of this business!

2. What MLM offers

As I said earlier, the MLM offers a business system so impressive that intermediaries that raise the product or service is avoided.

As you know, in a traditional business until the product or service reaches the customer passes through many hands, as are the wholesaler, the storekeeper, commercial, and finally the establishment itself that sells it to the customer, so that all they are increasing the value of the product or service and in the end the customer receives a much more expensive product as it left the factory.

With MLM all these steps are saved and therefore all those costs that raise the final product or service. For this reason, they can afford to offer products or services to customers at attractive prices.

This business system also saves advertising costs are own Independent Distributors who perform the work of the business and advertise products or services.

In addition, the system rewards you for giving the opportunity to work with other people in MLM, that is, if you offer the business to others also receive commissions. And this can make any Independent Distributor.

This is how impressive business MULTINIVEL: For business recommend you also receive a commission!

In addition, if they do exactly the same thing as you, recommend the product to others and help them thrive, you will also receive lifetime commissions.

How about? Is not it awesome?

You can recommend the business to as many people as you want.

Therefore, it is a matter of time and worked to obtain significant revenue each month.

Thus NETWORK YOUR ROOTS ARE MADE larger and therefore will be increasing your income. Everything is a matter of time and dedication.

The MLM business which offers a wonderful outlet in times of crisis. The key to success is to see it as a real business. I love you encourage you take it very seriously, because I know it works.

This business allows everyone to achieve stability, income, quality of life that are not comparable with the effort to be currently performed in any traditional job to reach the same goal and that in most cases does not satisfy us given the current employment situation.

Now let us see what are the most common mistakes people make when starting a company Multilevel, which makes many fail to achieve their goals.

3. What usually fail in MLM

If we identify why 90% of those who start in this business fail, we will be prepared to avoid falling into the same mistakes.

The business works, you know the system and certainly see it as an ideal business and that of course requires work. You never think it will be easy and fast. We must work to achieve results.

The difference is that as the amount of work and dedication will be rewarded invest a greater or lesser extent. This does not happen in traditional jobs where you work to cover the expenses of the month. Multilevel, the work you do for a few years can easily meet the requirements of a lifetime.

I have identified the factors that lead to failure in this business and I want to know very well not comets. These are:

❖ **Lack of knowledge about the product or service, as well as the characteristics of the business and not know to value**

Training about products or services, the business model and the company are essential for success. This is usually the most common mistake that many comment.

Most begin with great enthusiasm, because you have attracted the benefits offered and the business system and also look them good products or services, but are not willing to invest time in training, in order to get to know each product or service.

Any businessman knows that the foundation of your business is knowledge of the products or services you offer.

Most who start an MLM business, no entrepreneur mindset.

As it has been a very low investment, they not value what they have at their disposal. They are seen as mere Independent Distributors and not as entrepreneurs. Therefore, no effort.

Beware believe in this false formulated BUSINESS = investment money.

It is a misconception that it is simply a business buying and selling.

The deal offered is not something to waste and less in the era in which we are living, where it is relatively easy to create a network, hence the need for people such as technology and potential that exists through internet.

The main thing is to know very well the products or services because they are the foundation of your business.

You have to think as you would an entrepreneur. First you have to try the products or services that you are offering, to make sure they really work.

A good entrepreneur understands the potential of your business and working to increase results. He falls for their products or services. You can not give something you do not know or you use. That's clear.

A good businessman always perfect his work.

That is, analyzing the mistakes and learn from them, documented, invest much of their time in training, learn from others, implements the methods that work and works hard to achieve their goals.

A good entrepreneur knows that the difference between succeeding and not have to work is equal to or more than those who have achieved success.

If you do not have a multilevel entrepreneur mindset, failure is assured, unless what you want is simply to get a little extra income; for it does not take much effort.

But if you want consolidarte and achieve your goals you have to have vision of entrepreneur / a.

You have to see the business as your own company.

❖ Lack of knowledge of marketing, advertising and business dealings

Another problem that arises most multilevel entering, is the lack of knowledge of marketing, advertising or business deal.

Naturally, since this knowledge must be acquired. Certainly there are people who have communication skills and commercial innate and manage to achieve success for their skills and the attraction projected onto others. However, commercial advertising and marketing techniques can be learned or easily imitate.

Here the figure of good mentor or sponsor that will help you understand and apply the proper techniques arises. That's why I created this book so that you achieve success by applying a series of knowledge and business skills while you become a great mentor or sponsor in the future for your own team.

So put into practice what you learn and use the techniques I offer you, because you have to teach them to others soon.

- ❖ **Not be highly motivated and not believe in the potential of business**

Not trusting the enormous potential of the MLM business, some are discouraged by not getting the expected results quickly.

They are thought to multilevel lot of money very fast win and that's not reality, leading them to distrust this system, so that when they pass 2 or 3 weeks and do not earn what they expect will come down and leave to work.

MLM is a distance race; if you persist and you will be surprised when you get the results you will no longer leave. Unfortunately, many people start and have no goals or plan of work, so are discouraged because they do not know how to work or are not willing to be guided.

Many see it as one more way to earn extra income and little else.

They are influenced by the system and strive very little, because they think that the more effort you should do is in other work or prepare for a traditional job.

Simply they do not value it as a real means of financial freedom: Those who think so you their loss!

So you have to remember every day what motivates you to keep working. Faith in the ability of this business is essential.

You have to be clear that the business operates and depends largely on your attitude.

If you're not sure what you want to achieve and do not cultivate a positive attitude it is very easy to give up this business. You have to train yourself to never lose heart and visualize how your life will be when you have achieved success.

This race is long and you will find obstacles to overcome, especially with great motivation, remembering what your goal is and cultivating your positive attitude everyday. If you do, you will achieve what you propose and multilevel find a more rewarding job than you've ever imagined.

❖ **negative influence of others**

You start with all the enthusiasm in the world and comets your family and close friends you've started your own business network .... Get ready!

They'll bombard you with negative comments about the multilevel. They will say that you are cheating, which is pyramidal, products or services do not have quality, because they think that is subtracted to offer big discounts, you're no good for that which you seek a real job ... .etc.

Believe me all have told us the same thing when we started. Some have come down with those comments. If you do not know "digest" that kind of negative arguments that are not true, they can discourage you. It requires several aspects have clear goals and know what you're going to score.

If you let yourself be influenced by outside opinions it is impossible for you to achieve success.

It depends on your good training, knowing the correct answer to these questions and taking clear that although respond in the best way, everyone will give their opinion and think what you want.

You should also be clear that you can live very well with your business. But it depends on you alone.

Not to be angry with whom you say negative things, because they often have good intentions and above all due to the lack of knowledge on this subject.

I speak from my experience, trust business, with time and perseverance have demonstrated to all those who thought that way they were wrong. In fact, it is anecdotal later some of those who have spoken evil of business you are part of your team.

Then they'll tell you: It's you're lucky! It is yours! Is that...! Anything but recognize that you have worked hard and the business you work for it.

So remember, you should not get mad or bad when they try tomártelo to let him or speak negatively about what you do.

On the other hand, which also is doing is failing many negative climate that are around. News and general atmosphere are pessimistic. You talk to people and many have been schooled to this way of thinking. They are not able to succeed because they believe that there is no exit.

Be very careful not to allow that general attitude affects you. You have to have very clear goals. NO WAY OUT AND IS WORKING FOR POSITIVE AND CONSTANT. This book will teach you to deal with negativity and work positively.

❖ **Lacking daily work plan or follow**

You've made the decision to join this great industry now what? ... what you have to do? Where to begin? In this book I offer you a daily work plan. Your success depends on you to follow.

❖ **Poor economic management**

A very important issue is the proper money management. Remember you have to be entrepreneur mindset, so it is essential to manage money in your business.

The first rule is to separate our domestic business accounts. A practical way to know how much we are really winning with our business, we have an account exclusively for it, with which we all business related movements, so really know our profitability.

Many do not take control of what they are earning, nor are administered properly to keep track of your stock, business, sales, customers, distributors, monitoring etc. I'll teach you to do so you improve your results.

❖ Failure to follow the pillars of success

The pillars of success have an order that must be followed to succeed. If we skip the order, failure is assured. The order is as follows:

- ✓ Know the products or services
- ✓ Share the products or services
- ✓ Share business

This order is. First you have to know the products or services, thus get positive experiences from them and can offer them with enthusiasm and confidence.

When you check the results of the products or services in other people and you verify that the business works, you're ready to share the business. If you follow step by step you will verify that it works.

Do not make the mistake that comment a lot, pretending to start by offering business without even having offered a single product or service and without even being convinced that they are really good and who have not proven themselves; honestly it is like trying to build a house and start from the roof ... impossible right?

We have learned to identify major mistakes that many people who start in MLM.

Now, let's learn how to avoid them and thus ensure success in this industry.

4. How to Succeed in MLM

The first thing to do to succeed is to follow the training offered by your company.

You must let yourself be guided and acquire the necessary skills from the company offer the training.

5. Your business!

This business gives you total financial freedom. You will achieve step by step, with daily work and being persistent; there is no other way.

There is no failure, there is a lack of work and not rely or not believe is achievable, so take your mind those negative ideas. The bad moments that arise are you going to overcome.

Although these bad times will also come, I will prepare to face them, are part of the process to achieve success. A "no" will mean only a number, a probability that brings you closer to a "yes."

Remember that if you do not get a "no" is that you are not working. All tell us and we will continue saying "no". We already know. If everyone would like the products or services or make the business what would happen? Do you not seem impossible that everything was that easy? If it were that simple would not need to read anything here you expose any NETWORKER would be at the top. Not everyone is willing to try new products or services, or to start an MLM business, so do not expect that everyone tells you so.

We understand and assume, but we also know we need some tell us that "no" to get the "yes". It is a matter of probabilities. With more people speak more likely we are to be told "yes". Assume you have to go out and talk to people. Communicates you have both the products or services like business, one way or another, depending on whom you head.

You have before you a business that will offer a quality of life you will not find another job.

The opportunity is unique. You are now at a turning point in your life: change your future uncertain job total financial freedom.

You can continue looking for what does not exist at this time or start working on your future with one of the most profitable businesses and more quality of life in the world.

Your economic stability, your family, your children, your retirement, your quality of life and depend on you valuable time and constant work on track. This is the business of your life.

You will have the help of your team, a team of trained trainers and successful, but should work. This word does not like to hear people ... "work" sounds to do something nasty and binding. The work I show you is neither mandatory nor unpleasant. If you persist will be nice and yourself / to want to. Persist and you will succeed.

You must put aside shame and fear of "what people say".

One can only approach the future that awaits you with months or years of hard work. Do not you imagine! But it all depends on you see it certainly as **YOUR OWN BUSINESS GREAT**, the best you could start where you still have to learn a lot and where everyone would propose triumph sooner or later. So .. get even!

6. Knowledge about products or services

It is very important to know the products or services. Essential to succeed. You must invest time in studying them. If you want to be properly prepared you should take time to know well each product and service.

Since it is your business, you should enhance knowledge about products or services with more information you can get from Internet or books.

You have to fall in love with the products or services. Why is it so important? That are the foundation of your business. It allows you to speak frankly, while you prepare to help more people.

Plan your daily work you'll include time for training. If you follow it you become a great sponsor / a, prepared / a for sale and to help your own team in the future.

Do not miss any formations ON LINE, videoconferences organized by your company to learn more about the products or services. If you "unplug" these formations ON LINE you lose experience, knowledge and help you need.

So it's essential that you are involved and are aware of when and attend if you can.

Remember that you can also offer your experience and benefit and encourage others to comment on their experiences that will benefit you.

If you have in your city or nearby formations in training centers holding your company I advise that you go to train you. It will be the foundation of your future success and your own team.

Identify what you do best, your qualities and exploit it to the fullest.

Know your strengths and what you enjoy doing is key. I'll give you an example: you may not know anything about internet and yet be a very positive person and comunicativa..¡Explota those qualities! Do not waste much time on the internet with a medium not control, as the results would take much longer to arrive than if you use your personal skills. While learning new things is necessary, exploits you do best first. Take advantage of your qualities.

7. Knowledge about the company and the business system

You must know well the company and the business aspects because potential customers and distributors with whom you contact will ask you questions about it and you need to know it thoroughly to solve all your questions, so you get to earn your confidence and give a professional image.

8. Theoretical training and implementation

Training is important. Training and techniques to reach more people and the methods to do it properly. You will reduce greatly the possible failure if you follow the methods I show you.

I'll give you several options aa job that you know and choose the one that best suits your personality. If you want to increase your results and know well other methods need training.

In this book you will find them, but only the theory. Missing something you should do for yourself ... PUT IN PRACTICE !. If you learn a lot of theory but not put into practice, you will not achieve the results you expect. So to succeed is needed especially PRACTICE.

9. A great motivation and self confidence.

Companies offer motivation systems, coach and methods to keep a positive attitude.

I as a trainer, I also need to nurture a positive attitude every day. We are exposed to negativity "out there".

So we have to protect ourselves with motivation and methods that enhance our positive attitude. We have to continue training and cultivating, by reading a book, listening to audio or watching videos.

The book I recommend is PLENTY SUBCONSCIOUS, Removing subconscious blocks 3 money, a book written by NACHO MUÑOZ.

I do not get commission for offering this book, but as you're a person of action,'LL GET EASIER AS YOU CAN TOTALLY FREE, but you'll have to pay shipping charges.

In order to acquire this valuable book copy and paste this link:
https://www.juancarlosmartin.info/libroabundanciailimitada

Believe it or not, stay motivated and positive attitude is necessary for my team and for me and also for you. So start developing your motivation gives you the information in this book, while continuing to learn all about the business.

You must do it as natural and progressive way to go implementing the work plan.

Earnings employs well. Try to separate accounts for personal expenses business expenses. If you have two separate accounts you can enter the earnings in the account of your own business and cover business expenses such as Internet, telephone, stationery, etc. and so you can check the benefits you're getting.

We are talking about earnings. Remember that you still have the benefits of RESIDUAL COMMISSIONS intact or if you do network.

I advise you to take these suggestions into practice, it may seem cumbersome, but you'll make sure to keep your business alive

98

10. The time management

It is very important to manage your time well, it's gold. Whether you're a full-time part, you must organize well each activity.

You must devote time to family, business and yourself. If you're in business full time, you'll have easier; but if you're combining your business with your traditional job, I'll give you some tips:

Find yourself a work schedule that mark if possible appointments for hours. Tacha hours of your workday, your hours of daily activities with family or personal and choose how long the day you devote to your new business.

They can be 2 or 3 hours each day, it is recommended at least if you want to succeed in MLM. Please note that you will grow professionally and personally.

For example, if you are a person who used to go to the gym, karate class, soccer, English classes or activities kids if you have family, etc. write them down on your calendar so you do not desatenderás your activities or your family. Now, really how much time you have and how long you want to spend?

Also greatly influence your personal priorities, that is, there are people who take precedence recreational activities to a business presentation with a new guest, then you will have to assess your commitment to your business.

Ultimately, it is how much level of seriousness you want to put. Once decided above, schedule your appointments for business in the gaps that you have been released and have those interested in hearing you fit your schedule, not the other, because if you're the one who has to adapt to the times of others, you're wrong. You'll end up believing that this activity steals a long time, you're all day "pringado / a", etc. etc. and you abandon.

Remember, MLM or Network Marketing business is a distance race, not speed. Even if your boot should be explosive at first, then you must dose your effort for the endurance race.

11. Daily Work Schedule

You have to be disciplined with your daily work plan. You have to have some daily goals. Makes good use of your time and follow the plan that I offer in this book as well as the Company.

12. Display the goal

Your goal may be economic stability, earn income for life, have a comfortable retirement, working without bosses or schedules or just get some extra income.

All this can be achieved perfectly. Visualize your goal and work to achieve it. Spend a few minutes every day to visualize that you've achieved your goal. Displays the results and what you've accomplished. The free time you have, the income you can get to enjoy the quality of life you have obtained. Enjoy these moments every day and thus make it.

That said I will show you how to work on my computer.

13. School online

Everything is managed by communicating with the team.

This is what my team and I do ....

It is important that every time you sponsor a person within the team we do know so we can give you access to private training. This is because we need to control who has access to secure information.

We also want to greet and encourage that person who starts and record it in the system of formations and videoconferences ON LINE offer on your computer.

We get in touch with him to greet him and offer access and registration in our training system.

We discuss the training that we will offer in this school: start with training so that the company knows well (performance, products ...) then how to offer the business.

We will remind you should not miss training Videoconferences we do almost every week. TRAINING which are are private. They are exclusive to team members and do not give access to anyone, because we talk about sales techniques and working methods. This training is for the team.

There is also opportunity meetings in our video conference room, which can privately invite anyone who wants to know the business. That way they can grow their network.

In our team we also provide updated information on many aspects of business. Being registered in our private group of WhatsApp and Facebook, regularly receive by post information, ideas and help on aspects of business.

You can count on us. Eventually, they themselves will create their own team of Independent Distributors.

They will have to train them and therefore have to protect this training, it will also serve to train them. Remember that as you go sponsoring people on your team is essential that we communicate, thus the whole team is trained and they benefit from it.

We give them the opportunity to be part of the creative team JCM Digital Marketing.

Our team is open and we need help and collaboration. Everyone can be part of the creative team of this training. It requires hard work and demonstrate ability to help others. Only they need to provide useful and beneficial to the team training and post. If they do often involve and be part of this team.

For more information visit:

http://www.auladelexito.info/

That said we started training.

14. Products and Services

This is most important to your business: KNOW THE PRODUCTS OR SERVICES PERFECTLY. All the time you invest in knowing, for those who are suitable, etc. It is well spent. But most important it is to have experiences with products or services.

If anything they ask and not know the answer, do not worry, it's normal, because you just started. Please do not venture to answer a question without knowing the answer either. It gives confidence to say something like, "Sorry, but not know the answer to that question. I prefer to consult with the company and give you the best advice "before responding somewhat imprecise, lose the trust of that person.

Talk to your sponsor and see if he knows the answer to the question if it can not contact the company and making the request.

Eventually you can answer almost any question, although there are people who have spent years and prefer not to venture into unknown issues. it is best to be very cautious.

15. Arguments of the Products or Services

use: Using the products or services is the pillar of your success NUMBER ONE. Believe it or not if you do not use the products or services yourself / a success in this business is very difficult. It is true that you can sell any product or service. You may also sponsor someone, but little else ... I'm warning you right from the start: "If you are not in love with the products or services and if you have no experience with them TREASURY not go far".

It is the base, if you want to create a strong network you have to be a regular consumer of your products or services. If you want to offer them safely you have to know that are really good and have experiences with them. How will you train your network if you do not appreciate yourself based on your business?

Therefore, we recommend you start at the base: **KNOWS THE PRODUCTS OR SERVICES.** Go further and investigate accordingly. For example, you should be very familiar with specific details about the products or services to offer them safely.

Use the products or services as soon as possible: This advice I give to you to make and accumulate purchases products or services in your home. That would not be smart. What I want is you gain confidence that really the products or services are of the highest quality and have experiences with them. So begins as soon as possible using the products or services and offer them to your family.

Once you do, everything will be much easier. You can talk about them with enthusiasm. You can share them with freeness of speech. Those who speak to you notice you tell them the truth and they really want to help them based on your own experiences. This is fundamental.

You never feel like a salesman / a. Products or services are not sold ... what we do is cause us to buy them, but we do naturally based on some knowledge, arguments and most importantly experiences with products or services.

Share: Share the products or services is easy when you feel real enthusiasm for them. It's really easy if you own experiences and the knowledge that are unique.

Remove from your mind the idea that your business is based on selling products or services. This business moves by feelings. Focus on transmit sensations. Do not focus on selling, if not to report. A few more people you are able to inform throughout the day, the more success you will have. Measure your business for the amount of people who are reporting products or services, not for sale.

Nobody likes to sell us anything. That if we all like to buy something we think is good or necessary. When we are convinced that something is going to benefit, we want it and finally we bought it knowing it will certainly benefit us. So what we have to do to purchase products or services to us, is to report on its features and above all explain our own or close experiences with the product.

So Focus on properly inform and convey your own feelings. I repeat many times, because it is a fundamental key.

He thinks something happens to us all: When you meet a salesperson you put on the defensive is not it? All happens to us when we detect that the person talking to us he wants to sell a product or service.

We think that simply aims to make money. But it is very different when we noticed they really want to help, you know what they carry in hand and know the product or service that they have done really well.

In short: you have to convey your own feelings and simply dedicate to report. You must share what you have known, based on your own positive experiences with products or services.

Where do you start? Who do you have to think to offer products or services? It begins with those closest to you. Sit down, take your time to think about all those people you know. Now you've studied the products or services you can find out what people need. You are creating YOUR NEAREST LIST OF CANDIDATES. To create this list you have to think, for example, in:

- ✓ Family
- ✓ Current and former friends
- ✓ physical and mobile phone book
- ✓ Social networking contacts and email
- ✓ Current and former neighbors
- ✓ Workmates, school, courses, current and former.
- ✓ Traveling companions, gym, etc.

- ✓ Service providers. Also supermarket cashiers, gas stations, bakeries, hairdressers etc. where we usually go.
- ✓ All of the above applies to your partner and close family if we and supports us in this business.

At the end of the book you'll learn to download the memory game, you'll love to learn where to contact people at this time you can not imagine.

From this list of candidates you will begin your plan of action. With some you will contact directly with others by telephone and others you will contact via email. Must continually be adding names to your list. You also have to update it almost daily, to know when to return to try to contact some people who doubted start the business as well as record day contact and what was the conversation.

The list must make it grow every day. There is a phrase that you should always keep in mind: "In this business achieved success who have a larger list of candidates, not because they know more people, but because they chose to make the world A SOURCE OF CANDIDATES". You should contact everyone who can not prejudge.

Before contacting people on your list, identify the needs they have. If you know the problems they face and have a starting point from which. On the other hand, there may be people who need to earn extra money or who are unemployed.

Although there are currently a huge job insecurity, so it would be an advantage for them to start working on a plan "B" if everything fails, so this type of business is also ideal for them. Why not stay with them to talk about the business, focusing the conversation as that may interest them?

It could also be that you have to explain the products or services first and then business option.

Is probably now you're beginning have the feeling of being ridiculous. If you yourself / a ashamed to talk about the business do not expect to succeed. No negative offer something you think is good, both in products or services as well as in the form of business. So do not cut at all, because they're trying to help. If you do not listen they do not insist.

More questions to ask yourself: Do you need extra income? Are they going through economic hardship? .. Help them! Offer them business!

Do they have a secure job? Offer them a way to have a plan "B" if they fail the job.

Begin as soon as possible to generate their extra income and create their own network.

Dedicating a little time each week will begin to consolidate income for life. Let them know when the next meeting will OPPORTUNITY ON LINE in the room Videoconferencing equipment. Thus, you can easily sponsor who want to learn about the business opportunity.

How to share products or services? There is no concrete answer, it all depends on the person you are writing to. You should try to identify the best way to approach it. Sometimes you have to show enthusiasm, sometimes it is not necessary and simply display the arguments that make good products or services.

Other times, you have to wait arise during the conversation, the right time to talk about it. It is very important to listen to the other person and truly interested in what he says. There are unsuited to talk now, for perhaps the conversation about other matters and must leave the topic for another time. Do not burn your chances in bad times! Never show despair or rush. It is short and if you do not perceive interest, do not waste any more time or insist.

16. Arguments of this business system

Well you know the arguments to offer the business. Many, but these are the highlights:

- Products of the highest quality.
- Everyone knows and consume natural products.
- The greatest benefits of the market, we can make money in several ways.
- Most compensation residual.
- No purchase obligations. Only shop when you want.
- Quality of life for you and your family. (Better health and family life)
- You own your time. In this work you decide when and how to work.
- Without Bosses without timetables.
- Your income will increase each month. They are also heritable and lifetime.
- Quality training
- Facilities sponsorship OPPORTUNITY ON LINE JOINTS

These arguments must remember very well to explain and develop them in a conversation. Sometimes you do not need to show them all.

Once you feel ready to help others, it means that the time has come to offer the business. To know your readiness, do yourself some questions honestly:

Do I own or experiences very close to the products or services? Do use? Have I replaced my home products or services consumed by my business?

Have I earned money on direct selling?

Have I already made a first taste or presentation and I feel ready / a to teach to make a business presentation tasting or who is incorporated into my computer?

Could you answer simple questions about the products? Am I really ready / a to help a person to dealer do? How can I help you make money?

Have I proved to myself / to business is good because I have already had results for sale?

Do not forget that your immediate environment will not be dealer immediately. They're going to let time to see how will you. And perhaps want to see results within a few months, they will be decided based on your results. If they see you're still constantly and with courage, with clear goals, then you may decide that certainly is a good deal.

So it's best to go before them have obtained results and experiences. Show them that business is good and that the products or services work!

Everything will be easier if you speak honestly of your results and certainly the business is worth. Therefore, you must dedicate yourself to start to get results in own experiences and direct sales.

17. I give you some ideas.

The most effective are those that arise conversations without forethought. They usually start talking about the topic that everyone is talking now: the crisis. It is the ideal place to explain that you are very happy to have started work on one of the businesses that help overcome the crisis time. This will give rise to a good conversation.

You can also telephone them to be: Be kind, say hi to them and to the point with sincerity and enthusiasm. You can explain that you have begun to work with certain products or services and you've seen that really are good.

Talk about your own experiences. You see it is very important to have experiences. STRESSES THE SALES PITCH AND ESPECIALLY THE EXPERIENCES. Ideally abide still in person so we can talk face to face, you can appreciate your honesty. Is one day at a specific time. If you see fit, after the conversation you can send that person, by email, the website of the company, your promotional website or a sales letter like this:www.juancarlosmartin.info/aloevera/

We talked about the close circle of people you know. Remember that your LIST OF CANDIDATES must review it and work it every day. Then we offer you a daily work plan. Let us see how you can offer products or services to strangers.

In this section we will focus on delivering business to dependents and assistants of any establishment: Banks, Gift Shop, Newspapers, watches, stationery, laundry, bar, Hardware, Optics, etc .. Do not forget any establishment, unless they have a lot of work at that time and they can not serve you, in which case is to return another day.

The first is to keep track of business you visit. For this you must make a map of the area you want to work. It covers two or three blocks from establishments every time you go to offer products or services and business.

It is important to have the mindset ready to receive negative responses, as is usual. To do this you need to understand that to be successful on a visit you need to do at least ten visits where you say no. You must also assume that you'll have rejection, but also successful. Now you have no experience, so that rejection is more likely when you take two or three weeks to do so. The positive attitude is essential to success.

As you see, smile, positive attitude and of course go well groomed / a is very important. Always leave a good feeling in the people they visited.

Remember back in a reasonable time from 2 to 3 days to revisit. When we return them we will have a very positive question: "WHAT IS WHAT YOU LIKED?"

It is a daily work, which will give its fruit with effort and perseverance. They are making repeat customers and often. In many cases it is also easy to create your own network of independent distributors offering discounted buy directly from factory or even offering them get another form of income.

Important note: If you say they do not want anything, there is a very positive response and that will give very good results:

"I want to ask if you know someone responsible, that's a good person and hardworking, because we are offering work to people who want it. This paper works, because we have very good quality product at the best price. Customers when repeated test products, so if you know someone who has no work and have good qualities could visit and explain how this job works. "

If you get a phone number or say the following when contacting direction of the person: "I'm calling because I've been in this establishment ... Such a person has spoken highly of you told me that you are a responsible and hardworking person, and therefore contact you because we are offering a very good opportunity for self-employment. I would like to stay with you to explain better "

Deal: Offer the business to others is the basis of MLM business. A business where we have the best quality of products or services and huge profit margins, the largest in the market. It is a great pleasure to discuss our business with others.

Of course, as you begin to sponsor you must make a commitment to focus on helping your team.

There are several methods to offer the business to others. Then I show you some of the easiest ways to carry it out.

18. ways to offer business

Offer the business is also very nice. Helping others to earn income. But you do once you've managed to follow the steps above and not before, because you would commit an error, not being prepared / a to help your own team. If you're going to offer the business should be after you've been successful and when you have already seen the potential, but not give a convincing picture.

There are many ways to do this, it all depends on the type of people you go direct. I'll show you ways to do it properly with the different profiles of people.

To provide business for myself and my team, I have prepared an automated system to work automatically. You can see it inhttp://www.auladelexito.info/ It is a system applicable to any MLM business.

> **HERRAMIENTAS**
> CARTA DE VENTAS
> 1 SISTEMA EN PILOTO AUTOMATICO
> 3 LANDIN PAGE
> 1 FORMULARIO DE MAS INFORMACIÓN
> 28 MENSAJES PREDISEÑADOS Y PERSONALIZADOS
> 15 IMÁGENES
> 7 VIDEOS
> 1 EMBUDO DE MARKETING
>
> *Juan Carlos Martin*

Video response: Another way to respond, simpler is sending a promotional video explains where business and products or services are exposed.

Workplan: Your work plan depends on the time you have available to devote to the business. Some have only 1 or 2 hours a day, others will have all day.

Remember you have to focus on that with which you feel better. And gradually keep trying other things. You always have to learn from what you do best and profile and work on what is not giving you so well. It is to be as complete as possible.

The beam principle that with which you feel better. The easiest thing is to talk to people you know and then go enlarging the circle to strangers. In this business it is to enhance your innate qualities and gradually begin to acquire new knowledge and skills to exploit them. But first devote yourself to take advantage of what you enjoy doing and what more comfortable / a feel.

If you are a rather negative person, you need to motivate yourself every day. There are people who do not need much motivation, so you must analyze yourself well and know your strengths much to know which work and spend more or less time.

Maybe you only have time to do a few activities. Try to carry out all the things you propose the company, although devote less time you'll be practicing the methods that the other teams this worked.

What for some it is a working day for you may assume a week because you do not have more material time. Do not worry and continue with the plan as your means.

Discover what works best for you and put it into practice. If something goes well do not change. If something is not because you have to change something.

Analyze it and work on it to improve results.

Of course, more dedication better results. Everything is relative. So do not get discouraged and move on with the work plan that we will offer. Works! It all depends on you to put it into practice and your involvement in it.

19. Objectives

These are the goals you should marcarte and you can achieve.

<u>First fifteen days</u>:

- Have business cards

- Have you easy strategies your company

- Knowing the sales pitches perfectly and be able to explain to others

- Learn and practice the script tasting if you were to offer a product or presentation if you were to offer the business. If practice is necessary before a mirror a few times, until you feel good. The goal is to do as soon as possible or actual presentation tasting (can be your family and you can go read the script if it is not what you've learned) and be sure to attend at least six people

<u>From the first month</u>:

- Have already created your video presentation to send to whom you request information

- Have regular customers who already have visited other times

- Sponsor at least 2 people in your first month

- Tastings, demonstrations and presentation products or services business for someone your starting team

20. Training

Ongoing training is essential for everyone.

We recall again this point because it is very important. Yourself and your team of distributors need training.

You and your team you are interested in being connected to the training system. Regarding the training and opportunity meetings to make your company in the videoconferencing room, we recommend that you attend and you notify your team to recordárselas and encourage them to attend. If you are involved / them also be involved. Your team is an extension of yourself.

If you keep you updated and is constantly working them from becoming infected likely that this attitude to them.

So stay tuned to your e-mail always where you receive information about upcoming meetings open to the public opportunity and FORMATIONS private and novelties.

They will also inform the new material will offer your company and your team to help in the sale and promotion of your business. If you like to share ideas, methods and help you work and you want to share with all your team, do it. All contributions will be valued positively.

Then we will see the different methods that we can continue to receive training and systems.

Opportunity meetings online: Its purpose is to help you easily sponsor. JOINTS OPPORTUNITY ON LINE aim to invite others to become distributors.

Anyone who knows the access can see them from your home. They are live and informs them about the sales pitch with each of the products as well as the reasons why it is worth doing business. The person performing exposure on the board of opportunity will always be someone with a lot of experience, so you can relax invite others to attend.

It is your responsibility to contact the person you have invited after Opportunity Meeting to answer any questions you may have. You can ask: What do you like best?

MODULE 4
Tips that will lead to success in network marketing

1. The importance of choosing a company and a good Mentor

For success in your MLM Business, one of the most important factors is the choice of a good Multilevel, a leader who will help you develop your business efficiently and grow as a person FOMA simultaneously. You must have the following considerations:

The work team: You must be connected to your willingness to work, it is vital to ensure your success in Multilevel Marketing.

Willingness to work Many people will seek only a good sponsor to make them work and they "live the story" that is not so, has never been and will not work if something caught my attention when I met MLM years, was the conviction that had most people, of getting some sort of obligation to the first person who told you about the business, so if sooner or later you consider this opportunity you find interesting, you join the team this person.

That suits your profile: The person who offers the first business suits profile person with whom you work when you like, you feel comfortable and can bring you what you need to develop your business. However, not all cases this happen, and for peace of mind telling you that you should not feel any obligation to this person or to any, since your future and your dreams depend on it greatly, and that's all and what is truly important.

That can help your sponsor: Ask yourself always, what can help this person, if you have some quality that you admire and want to learn, and be very careful and cautious when choosing with whom you are in your business, do not risk your financial freedom and your dreams. This is basic believe it or not ... and you'll see from time even if you do not.

Some useful tips when evaluating person and / or team want to join:.

- Look great in the way he has contacted you, in your overall attitude: since no one can give what he does not have an unprofessional person can ever teach you to be. .

- Never a someone who uses a job you do not like it, because this system will be that you will recommend follow you, which means you're going to have to work unwillingly, or get you life for your account. .

- Above the theme of work, you must always take into account the personal side, a good leader is someone who cultivates and strengthens personal development, so that growing as a person can help others to do so too. .

- If your idea is to work from home, you need to join a team to control and dominate all the tools that are currently available for work online, they can transmitírtelo whatever your level of computing, that is, other than a valid only for expert system. You need to be an effective, and easy to learn and use. Until you find all these circumstances, keep looking, your choice is an important part of your success.

2. It depends only on you

MLM success depends on you

Did you thought that the person to whom you offered the business opportunity thought you would earn more than herself?

Me. With this wrong thinking, actually they think that the success of your business depends on your decision. Well, if everyone rejects your opportunity would be so, but that's literally impossible.

Why? Why You'll also find many people who are like you, who also will be attracted by your business opportunity.

Remember how you felt when you were offered the business

When you think you do not succeed, it is good to remember the feeling you had at the time you reported business and you realized the potential that you had before. How did you feel?

Is not that saw a promising future ahead? Do not forget that you have at hand to millions of people who are like you, who also understand the business model, and will not have prejudices. People also will capture potential business if you get to them. It is only to find them, and that if it is up to you.

Win over who else is working for your team

I never get tired of saying it: In a MLM business that works longer and more skills acquired to help your team is the one that will have more growth. It will not win you more business presents, if not yourself, if you really want to work and you acquire skills. If so earn more than your sponsor.

So if you give to people who think that you have more to gain than themselves ... discard them in one fell swoop. Seriously, they are not suitable for your business. If after presenting information clearly, they still have prejudices do not waste time. Still looking for people like you. Your success does not depend on others depends on finding people who are right, they see it as you and believe me, there are many to be found.

Continues to offer the business and bring with them. That's why I say it depends on you. Continues to offer your business and find them.

3. Define your goals and your dreams

A dream come true!

It was six years ago behind a bar a restaurant and now I will celebrate my 6 years as a consultant and advisor to Digital Marketing.

I have to confess that even in my wildest dreams I imagined that scenario.

Now I realize that a great dream transform into a strong reality and for that I suggest 7 steps to accomplish any project:

- 1- Having a vision - Where you want to go
- 2- Have an action plan - How will you get
- 3- Have a specific date - The difference between a dream and a project it is the date.
- 4- To analyze the resources that accounts - Be creative to get them.
- 5- imperfectly Action Do not wait for everything to be perfect to try it, just create it.
- 6- Have patience - Do not expect the easy way, be patient and generates resistance meantime.

- 7- Do not be overcome by the comments of those around you - Many will tell you it's impossible, you dedicate yourself to make it possible.

No matter what time of your life you are, seeks to reach contradict the negative voices, the mediocre, jealous of your dreams, the one who you want to steal your peace. No one, absolutely no one interrupts your life project, you have been born for something very big and God in His infinite wisdom put it right there in your heart. Now it's up to heaven reclaim what heaven has given you.

Find your hopes, dreams and constrúyelos paint them with faith.

4. Excuses for not starting a business

Countless people who crave a business, they want to be independent or work from home. Sleep is wonderful, however there are also many who fail even before trying.

- "It was not the time"
- "It's that I could not raise the money"
- "It had no support"

Does it sound familiar to you? Today I share most common excuses for not undertake and how to overcome them. Surely you must eject it from your thoughts and take a step further with determination to achieve it.

- **I do not know how to do it.** Learn!
- I have support from my family. You do not need.
- I have support from my friends. Nor you need.
- I do not know how to start. Reads a lot and learn.
- I do not put business. Find something you like and know how to do.
- can not do anything. Studies or learn something.
- I have no money. Save!
- **I'm bad to save.** Apply for a loan.

- **I'm bad with credits.** Seeking an investor for your family.
- **I'm afraid to borrow.** Save.
- **I've never sold anything.** Learn about sales and then try.
- **will not sell.** The worst that could happen is that you do not buy.
- **I do not want to sell.** Hire sellers.
- **I do not like dealing with people.** You must learn.
- **I do not have patience.** Hire an administrator.
- **I am messy.** Seeks support with someone who is ordained.
- **Not handle money.** Hire an administrator.
- **I do not know where to start.** Planned.
- **Not as planned.** Start by writing your ideas.
- **It makes me fear losing my money.** Worse never try.
- **It gives me fear failure.** If you do not try, you've failed.
- **I do not want to lose my job.** Do not give up yet and start small.
- **I have no time.** Planned for later.
- **I have many commitments.** Start small.
- **I have a lot of debt.** That is the aim of undertaking.
- **I'm alone.** Many women have started their own large businesses.
- **I have a baby.** Your baby should be your motivation is not your excuse.

- **I have many economic problems.** Your business will help them.
- **My boss will not like me to go.** Your boss will not feed your children.
- **I worry about not knowing what to do.** Along the way you learn.
- **I still worried about not knowing what to do.** Seeking advice.
- **What if things go wrong?** If something goes wrong have a plan B.
- **What if I lose my money and my job?** You try again or find another job.
- **I do not like dealing with employees.** You know that is part of the process.
- **What if employees are bad?** Hire the best.
- **What if employees steal me?** It establishes good controls.
- **Not sell that product.** It distributes something that is in demand.
- **And if the market is saturated.** Innovates and sells something that is in demand.
- **And if it is not sold.** Looking for another product.
- **And if customers fail.** If you do a good study come.
- **And if you do not like my product.** What improvements and try again.
- And if there is a lot of competition. It is because you're in an attractive market.
- **And if there is unfair competition?** Be creative and fight.

- **I do not feel safe undertaking.** Studies and prior to start planning.
- **I am very afraid to try.** Planning combat fear.
- **Not when you take the plunge.** When you have planned enough.
- **What if the economy comes under.** Like your job would also be at risk.
- **I'm afraid to risk my money.** If you plan properly the risk is lower.
- **I'm afraid not know how to handle success.** Surely you learn.

As you can see, each argument has an output. So you look no further excuses to take your business, dismisses this list and get to work. You will see that energy, creativity and planning results and satisfactions come.

5. mentality Multilevel

It is to have a multilevel mindset

Not everyone is ready to start a MLM business. To most people lack the mindset of an entrepreneur, or as I say, multilevel mindset.

Hostelero have been for 10 years and have always liked to measure the potential of a business to consider well the factors involved. When I started I saw numbers and what could be achieved in income and quality of life. I started very seriously and now I have no financial problems and enjoy quality of life.

These are the numbers I did and I found that I passed believe.

I thought I could build 6,000 euros with one month of work. Actually more than that.

You think if I told you that you can generate more than 6,000 euros a month. Trust me! It is not difficult: Generate 6,000 euros in one month of work. Totally true.

But to understand it must be seen as follows: If you consolidate income, for example 50 euros per month per month in a year will be 600.

50 x 12 months = 600 euros per year

Avanza 10 years from now. 50 x 10 years = 6,000 euros in 10 years.

With the effort a month you are generating 6,000 euros to perceive over the next 10 years and this is just one example, because the life of a good MLM company is unlimited, and you also have set an example with a reduced amount.

Remember that are consolidated revenues: consolidated- 50 this month, 100 the next, 150 the next, and so the entire time you're working. To understand this we must have a multilevel mindset, ie, businessman or businesswoman.

But, of course, you need income now. ALREADY! You're not willing to wait many months to live fully consolidated with the business. What can you do?

To this are companies that offer besides good business multilevel offer you the chance to make money by selling products. If you are good products are price, quality and people use will be easy to offer.

But you must have a major selling benefit. Thereby combining to provide direct sales business opportunity (create network) you get to live in this business in a few months.

You are seeing these numbers you know if an MLM is interesting or not for you.

6. Define your identity

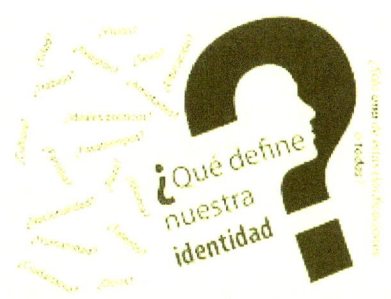

If you are in MLM you must have to stay clear your identity. Your turn to take a well-defined unless you're just here just to earn extra income decision.

But if you did not come to play, that is, really want to get real financial freedom you must take the step now log in with your MLM business.

Define your identity

I explain what happened to me: I was a hotelier for 10 years, owner of the company.

When I discovered the potential of network marketing I realized that was what I wanted to do. my former profession of hotelier is over.

Since then, he no longer told people it was INNKEEPER was clear about my identity. In a few months living exclusively MLM business, and

I'm sure that if I had not taken that step would not have had those results.

If he had doubted he would be projected on others who do not really trust in the potential of MLM. I myself would predisposition to failure. And everyone would convey indirectly that I am in network marketing only to earn extra, or have nothing better.

That is the positive or negative impact that will create if you do not identify clearly.

That's why I encourage you again: Define your identity clearly. As soon as you have decided and hit full.

Most multilevel has not defined its identity

Many people are retracted, perhaps just starting out and have no business experience. Also they do not want to throw away years of career, or profession or previous experience. They wonder: "What if I convey to people the idea that no longer need a job ... and reason:" So if anyone knows of any job will not think of me, you will not tell me ... "

If you think like multilevel business you are only going to give you extra as much. But you're not going to get very far. Probably you abandon in a few months.

Clearly, something is wrong: Either you do not have clear business potential, or the company in which these, or you're not sure you want to leave your job.

If you take a decision prove it every day

If you do decide to leave behind previous activity and focus on the multilevel not play. It works 100% every day. You can not define your identity half. The consequences for your business from your decision can mean financial freedom, extra, or a waste of time.

If you define your identity and decant the multilevel forward, but works every day. This is a race of endurance, not speed.

Many start with a lot of speed and then get tired.

Informaciom hope this makes you reflect and make a well thought out decision, but once taken go for it!

Again I ask the question: Are you here to earn extra or you come to stay? Your decision will depend on your results. I hope you're clear.

1. As offering your company as project or as an opportunity

Offer the business at the time and do it properly.

Offer the business is also very nice.

Helping others to earn income. But you do once you've followed the steps above and not before, because you would commit an error not be Prepare @ to help your own team. If you're going to offer the business should be after you've been successful and when you've already proven the potential.

There are many ways of doing it; It all depends on the people you are writing to. You must do it properly with the different profiles of people.

Knowledge about the company and the business.

You must know well the company and the business aspects that you are going to ask prospective customers and potential distributors with whom you contact.

Training and practice, not only training.

Training is important. Training and techniques to reach more people and methods to do it properly. You will reduce greatly the possible failure if you follow a method.

If you want to increase your results and know well other methods need training. But not only the theory. Missing something you have to do ...: TO IMPLEMENT !. If you learn a lot of theory but do not put into practice you will not achieve the results you expect. So to succeed is needed especially PRACTICE.

Great motivation and confidence in you.

We are exposed to negativity "out there". So you should protect yourself with motivation and methods that enhance your positive attitude. You have to keep your attitude was forming and growing, perhaps reading a book or listening to audio or watching videos. Believe it or not it is necessary for you and for all. So your motivation starts to develop information and keep learning all about business.

We do not recommend buying products in order to obtain greater discounts. Remember that the products takes little time to get home from the order, so that no bunching. It is to make it as natural and progressive way that you implementing the work plan, either for personal consumption. Let yourself be advised by the person who sponsored you to know which products are the best sellers, if you want to have a small stock available in your home.

You might decide to buy some of the best-selling star product to keep on hand for sale and for own consumption. If you do keep in mind this rule of thumb: Replenish your intake. Some people do not put into practice this rule, if you do not replace the amount of your consumption every time you notice that you have less stock, and there will come a time when you will not have stock because you have eaten your business, and you'll Compel @ to have to make another effort to invest in products for your customers. Remember that your consumption is for your health and also part of business success, as have experiences with the products will greatly facilitate the sale, so do not see it as an expense, but as a way to gain health and sales.

Another important rule is to separate the amount it costs us products with sales gains. To do so notes in a notebook (or database) these signs:

- Date of sale
- Customer name
- Products sold in that sale

- PVP
- Dealer price and profit margin.

The date will need to know when you buy that customer products (as durability thereof) and contact the person again. The ideal question you must make when contacting is this: WHAT IS WHAT do you think? It is a positive question that facilitates a positive response. always remember it.

Rightly profits. Try to separate spending accounts for the cost of other things. If you have two separate accounts you can enter the earnings in the account of your own business and cover business expenses such as Internet, telephone, stationery, etc .. and so see the benefits you're getting. We're talking about gains in product sales. Remember that you still have the benefits of intact if you do RESIDUAL network. I advise you to take these suggestions into practice, it may seem cumbersome, but you'll make sure to keep your business alive.

Time management.

It is very important to manage your time well, they say it's gold. Whether you're a full-time part, you must organize well each activity. You must devote time to family, business and yourself. If you are full time, you'll get easier, but if you're combining your business with your traditional job, I'll give you some tips:

Find yourself a work schedule that mark if possible appointments for hours.

Tacha hours of your workday, your hours of daily activities with family or personal and choose how long the day you devote to your new business. They can be 2 or 3 hours each day, it is recommended at least if you want to succeed in MLM. Please note that you will grow professionally and personally.

For example, if you are a person who used to go to the gym, karate class, soccer, English classes, or children's activities, etc. write them down on your calendar so you do not desatenderás your activities or your family. Now, really how much time you have and how long time you want to spend? Also depend very much your personal priorities, that is, there are people who take precedence dance classes to a product or business presentation with a new guest, then you have to evaluate your commitment to your business.

Ultimately, it is how much level of seriousness you want to put. Once decided above, schedule your appointments for business in the gaps that you have been cleared, and make those interested in hearing you fit your schedule, not the other, because if you're the one who has to adapt to other times, you're wrong. You'll end up believing that this activity steals a long time, you're all day "pringad @", etc. etc. and you abandon.

Remember, MLM or Network Marketing business is a distance race, not speed. Even if your boot should be explosive at first, then you must dose your effort for the endurance race.

8. Here are some ideas for direct sales of products of Health and Welfare

The most effective are those that arise conversations without forethought. They usually start talking about the topic that everyone is talking now: the crisis. It is the ideal time to explain that you're very happy to have started work on one of the businesses that help overcome the crisis. This will give rise to a good conversation.

Another great conversation which would provoke you with your positive attitude.

People are surprised to see someone who is happy these days. And if you've managed to lose weight, or if you have passed a health problem or simply if you're careful, if you take care of your skin, people will notice that you feel good.

You can also telephone them to be: Be kind, say hi to them and to the point with sincerity and enthusiasm. You can explain that you have begun working with natural products and you've seen that really are good and quality. Talk about your own experiences. He explains that are natural and everyday. They have good price and you can even get them at factory prices. You see it is very important to have experiences.

STRESSES THE SALES PITCH: Stamps quality, origin, no parabens, etc.And ESPECIALLY experiences. Ideally it abides still in people so they can deliver some samples and a catalog given to test products. Is one day at a specific time. If you see fit, after the conversation you can send by email a catalog or refer to the website of the company through your dealer code so you can check the products we have.

We've talked about your closest people you know circle.

Remember that your LIST OF CANDIDATES must review it and work it every day. Then have a daily work plan. Let us see how you can offer products to strangers.

In this section we will focus on delivering products dependent and saleswomen of any establishment: Banks, Gift Shop, Newspapers, watches, stationery, Laundry, Bar, hardware, optics, etc .. Do not leave any establishment, not unless they have a lot of work at that time and they can not serve you, in which case is to return another day.

The first is to keep track of business you visit. For this you must take a map of the area you want to work. It covers two or three blocks of establishments for each time you go to offer products. It is important to have the mindset ready to receive negative responses, as is usual. To do this you need to understand that to be successful on a visit you need to do at least ten visits where you say no. You should assume that you're going to have rejection, but also successful. Now you have no experience, so that rejection is more likely when you take two or three weeks to do so. The positive attitude is essential to success.

As you see, smile, positive attitude and of course, go well arreglad @ s it is very important. Always leave a good feeling to people who visited.

Remember back in a reasonable time from 2 to 3 days to revisit. When we ask them a very positive question: "WHAT IS WHAT YOU LIKED?"

It is a daily work, which will give its fruit with effort and perseverance. They are making repeat customers and often. In many cases it is also easy to create your own network of distributors offering discounted buy directly from factory or even offering them obtain another form of income.

Important note: If you do not want to say anything is a very positive response and that will give very good results.

"I want to ask if you know someone responsible, that's a good person and hardworking, because we are offering work to people who want it. This paper works, because we have very good quality product at the best price. Customers when repeated test products. .for it if you know someone who has no job and has good qualities could visit and explain how this work. "

If you get a phone number or say the following when contacting direction of the person: "I'm calling because I've been in this establishment ... Such a person has spoken highly of you, you told me you're a reponsable and hardworking person, and therefore contact you because we are offering a very good opportunity for self-employment. I would like you to explain it better be "

You might find people who tell you they have no money. At this point there is to know if the person really wants the product or if it is an excuse. You can tell that there are ways to get them cheaper, but would recommend a simple: You can offer you organize a meeting or TASTING HOGAREÑA with sales to get the products and so you can buy discounted products.

It is absolutely necessary that you learn to do firesides. You get good income and customers for life and will prepare for many other aspects of business.

9. 10 Tips to invite a Network Marketing Business

1. Recognizes that need to learn and be teachable invite (you're probably acostumbrad @ to invite your friends, relatives or acquaintances a few beers, but you're not used to invite to know a business opportunity, therefore, first it is to have enough humility to let yourself teach).

2. Learn from those who are most successful (if the person who sponsored you directly does not yet have enough experience in the business, sure to find some leader in your upline who is willing to teach you).

3. Follow the system established by your company's success. Attends all training events in your company (and learn the system established success)

4. No Innoves (only geniuses innovate, and based on the premise that none of us are geniuses, it is much more sensible to copy or duplicate what do people who are already successful).

5. Set aside time each week to call your contact list (depending on your circumstances, devote more or less time, but to succeed, you will need to dedicate

at least 1 hour a week to invite your contacts in order to make business presentations every week).

6. The call will be very short (success in your call will be inversely proportional to the amount of things that you count on the phone: the more you talk, the less likely you are to that person to attend a presentation). Do not explain the business never by phone (like Ismael, a friend of mine, we call on an invitation, not a "invitopresentación" he says, because that term did not even exist in the dictionary ...).

7. Create curiosity and urgency in your call. At this eighth point, I need to put a few practical examples which I quote below: 10 Keys to learn how to invite the Network Marketing.

• "Hello! I just found the business that we can finally develop together without leaving our current work. I need to see you as soon as possible to explain the details. "

• I just started an activity / business very interesting, I would love to develop with you. When we will meet? Tomorrow or last?

• I just started a business on-line with a lot of potential to generate extra income, and I need you to give me your opinion. Can we meet this afternoon 40 minutes?

• He was about to leave, but I need to talk to you about an important issue, when you have 40 minutes?

8. Do not solve doubts and questions by phone (without realizing it, the end will have "shredded" badly business and your contact will no longer come to the presentation and therefore does not have all the information necessary to take their own choice). So if you ask questions, you can reply

Of course I will explain all the details, do not worry !. So I want to stay with you to see us personally. When you told me then that we are? Tomorrow or last?

• Business I do not like talking on the phone. I need to see you 40 minutes to give you all the information / documentation for this project. What time do we then see, at 18 or 19 h.?

• I do not have time now to explain (I have another call, meeting, go out ...). I need to see 40 minutes I give all the details of the project.

• Although a minority, you can find a contact to tell you that if you do not give details over the phone, will not go to the presentation, in which case it may be good to say the following: 10 Keys to learn how to invite the Network Marketing

• Do not worry, I called you because I think it's something that will interest you much, but if you do not want are left, nothing happens. But do not say I did not tell you ...

• Almost everyone, to the phrase "do not say I did not tell you" usually respond with: Come, okay, when we are then ?.

9. Show enthusiasm and determination. It is much more important how you say things, what really say. Or put another way, more importantly your environment, your content in the call.

10. Always keep high the opportunity. Never beg. If you pray, all you get is that person attends presentation of pity, and I assure you that this is not the way to get a committed partner. Plantéatelo the opposite: if you have him or her an opportunity to offer, I would be doing you a favor and then you would hear him, but if he or she has nothing to offer you, you who are doing a favor to that person, as you have in your hands, the opportunity that can change the future of that person and his family. Therefore, always keep high your chance.

10. In this you had not thought

Multilevel personal growth
Rarely it talks about the other benefits of a Network Marketing business, and believe me it's really important: I mean the personal growth you will experience in this profession.

Personal relationships
No doubt you'll improve relationships with others. You will realize face actions, personal interviews hundreds and even thousands. You're going to relate to people of different profiles, you will have to adapt, learn to listen, show empathy and understanding. This is very positive for other aspects of life, do not you think?

Overcoming
I am sure that you will carry out actions that will make you out of your comfort zone, which will give you sense of achievement and improvement.

You will realize that you can get where you propose, you have no limits and you can really improve yourself every day. This is a fantastic learning multilevel personal growth that will help other areas of your life.

Keep a positive attitude
This aspect of your personal growth in MLM is very important.

Since I started in this business for me has been a school of mentality and positive attitude to move forward despite any obstacles. I remember very well the motivational audios listening in the car and some videos or books about positive attitude have been very important for me in many aspects of life.

In a world that pushes us toward the negative it is essential to know techniques to change a day that seemed bad in a very positive day. That'll learn in Network marketing, since you're going to enter into a wealth of information on positive attitude and mindset that will help a lot, believe me it is so.

Teamwork and leadership
One aspect to value for your personal growth in MLM is teamwork. You are about to introduce a team, working methods and will have to adapt. In addition soon you have your own equipment and can help them. You'll have to learn to lead a team and joint action. Do you think it will be positive? Undoubtedly yes.

Marketing and publicity
If you belong to a team trained you will meet the latest marketing and advertising, both onsite and online. Marketing is a changing world and need to be updated. What today gives results within a few months stops working, so you need your team to learn what tools and methods can work at all times. That will serve for any action you want to perform.

Continuous training
You will also be trained to handle a web, to work in social networks, to graphic design, something so essential in the visual world in which we live. All these aspects will know if you want to advance your business and ultimately will experience great personal growth in multilevel.

Surely you will experience great personal growth if you develop a MLM business. Believe me it is one aspect that hooks. I can assure you that before starting this business was not going to learn so much, and you never stop learning.

How about? Is it worth the Network Marketing? Only these aspects that I have shown you here deserves it.

Every time we are more of us in multilevel and increasingly is becoming more known Network

Marketing. Give yourself a chance and start your own business with many advantages, including personal growth.

11. Multilevel sell products to friends

Are you worried multilevel selling products to friends, your surroundings, family and acquaintances? Many people hold back from starting a MLM business because they believe it mandatory to sell to the environment. Actually there is nothing binding in the way you develop your MLM business.

But what is certain is that these prejudices are limiting and not very well founded. So in this post I'll show you how to break those barriers that limit your MLM business.

What is the real problem

What is the problem we face? The problem is we do not want that somehow our relationship with the people we know, with our family, and our friends are affected. "What will they think of me? Do they think that I want to take advantage of them?"

So let's see 10 principles that will make you feel totally free to talk to anyone environment, friends, family etc about your products.

Ask yourself the right question

The question to be resolved is this: WHAT CAN I DO TO NOT AFFECT THE RELATIONSHIP, to think ill of me, or that I want to take them?

Express to your concern and tell. In conversation ... let her know you're worried about precisely who thinks ill of you, you do not want to think you're taking advantage of friendship somehow. If you talk to her it's because you think it's a good thing you have to offer and why ask me to tell you if it will feel like to know it and not talk about it. Undoubtedly the most important thing is to preserve and strengthen friendship, so these showing respect if you do so.

Talk about your experience with the products of your MLM company. Everything must from there. Why it's so important to start by having experiences before going to talk to others. The first pillar of success is key before talking to anyone.

Speak honestly and from the heart. You must be you. Do not give the appearance of following a typical script vendor. People do not like to feel like a fool when they are trying to convince of something. Speak with complete sincerity.

Focus on the need of the person. That is the main reason to talk to your friends. Think of a two products that could be interested by a personal need to have it or at home. Do not go to offer the entire catalog of your company. Only one or two products that you consider necessary for the person.

Gives a product or delivering test samples. Multilevel companies often have samples, so that shares these samples and also some products that you use with the person. That way you let check the results offered by the product and decide if you want or not.

Offer him the possibility of having the same discount you have. Explain that if you like the products you can have exactly the same discount as you have, then you can connect it to the factory as you are. So you're not taking a higher position, but you put it in your same situation.

Delivery additional product information you will provide. Delivery data sheets and printed information websites prestige on components of the product and its benefits. So you have more confidence in what you say.

Is not all with the sale. Even if you buy products Be determined to track a few days. Call her to see how it is, that this is going product. Shows that it really is your friend / a because you're worried about the person, it is not simply to sell and go. So friends act.

Be considerate. If you contact a person and is not the right time waiting for a better time. Note circumstances. Sometimes it is not the best time to do it. Wait for a better time and meets the needs of the time you have your friend / a.

Ten commitment to demonstrate your friendship although the sale will not occur. Strengthens ties ... You buy products or take actions to strengthen ties, for example, it is to take something, to get together, invite to eat your house, etc .. if you really prove it worries affect friendship.

If you consider these 10 principles you can have a clear conscience that your relationship is not going to be affected. On the contrary, it can even be further strengthened. Really they are limiting beliefs that prevent us from doing many things, that when we analyze and consider the problem is easy to find solutions and even turn around, as you saw.

12. If you only looking for money you will not be happy

Do not believe all the publicity they send us. There are also liars in this industry who will tell you you're going to sheathe doing nothing.

I leave an explanation that you will clarify everything. I hope you like it and help you avoid scams so common internet:

MULTINIVEL IN SPAIN

Increasingly companies in Spain Multilevel marketing are making a promising riches, suggesting that multilevel is easy to become a millionaire. That kind of Multilevel Marketing in Spain sounds like a hoax. The Spanish do not like to promise you castles in the air. Here we like to be truthful, seriousness and logic. Rich promises us do not work in Spain, we sound misleading.

Too many lies and promises pyramid in the world to believe that we are going to make millionaires easily into a MLM business or any other business cost. This promise with pictures of cars and houses, "successful people" have so that you get into your business and pay the huge fee for access. Nothing more than that.

The 'secret' MLM SUCCESS

Another way to promote the lies that is, "I have the secret", "was the formula that can make you a millionaire in your MLM business"

It is true that internet is changing continuously and sometimes certain system works best. At the end of the day, when you discover you realize that nothing is enduring. And it's not as profitable as they promise. There are incredible secrets. And if something works, you soon will everyone and no longer be a secret. Do not you think?

WHAT DO YOU REALLY A BUSINESS MULTILEVEL?

That is the question that must be done if you are going to devote to develop a MLM business. In my case I am seeking financial freedom. This is manage my time and work the way I decide as I want and my business running even when not present. I was without work and without future. I wanted to escape the insecurity of the labor market we have in Spain. I did not want to have more heads or schedules. And it has been a blessing to find the business that currently developing, as I have achieved the goal.

One example is the publication viewing the hize a Wednesday morning after having a coffee in a cafeteria. Meanwhile my business was growing.

That's financial freedom and that is to have a successful business from my point of view.

HAPPINESS NOT GIVING MONEY

Money is necessary, and we need to live in that we all agree. But wanting more and more and never have limit to accumulate money, possessions, cochazos and houses is a pathetic goal that unfortunately many people have put. They have been proposed to be millionaires and literally die in the attempt. Some succeed at the expense of destroying their family life and values. And if they do so honored, they realize that they are no happier than before. Then they have another worry: Keep the standard of living. And what about what we can not control but we want? Diseases and unforeseen us or our loved ones events.

By this I do not want to be pessimistic, if not realistic. Do not get into a MLM business to get rich or wealthy because you think you'll be happier if you succeed. Ponte realistic goals and fighting behind them. Those yes you can get them. Financial freedom is a realistic goal in multilevel in Spain and in any other country.

Meanwhile, enjoy the gift of life and use the time you have to do things that edify others and give real purpose to your life.

13. How to get support from your family

At first, what your family sees is that every time you are less at home and that bring little income to justify it: little money and less of you.

It is not fair to ask for support and understanding if you are not producing.

Bring results home and see your family begins to trust what you do and truly believe that everything you talk makes any sense. Show them that you strive and spending less time with them is not in vain.

Above all, give realistic expectations. If you're going to an event, do not disappear without further ado, let them know:

"Honey, I made the decision to achieve extraordinary results with this company and want you to know something. The next 12 months will be loathsome, tedious, they will be horrible. I will work 16 hours a day, almost without rest. I'll burn my boats and not look back. Practically I will not be at home, and 90% of the time you're at it, you'll spend on the phone. But I want you to know that I do it for us and it will be worth it. I promise to bring the results we need to change our lives completely. "

SALT AND NOW THERE IS TO PRODUCE AS YOU HAVE PROMISED! I assure you that if you spend 12 months in which you have not been working as should ... now that they will not understand. If you go all, you go all in every way.

Yes, stop deceiving yourself. If you really want to be a mere consumer, Selo. But no proclamations that will beat all records of precocity in the ranks of your company or yourself if you think to yourself to go even try.

How you'd pay someone for doing what you did for your multilevel marketing business last month?

It's an amazing question for you to realize if you're really producing what you should or what you would like ...

Lot of people would not pay another a single penny! If you're one of those ... Come on! You are your own boss. No one but you can revive your business.

14. Attention !! beware dreamthieves, not to steal your freedom

Cuidado con los MIEDOS les encanta robar sueños

When presented with a new project in front of us are always exhaltados of hope, joy, desire, strength, etc ... but we have to be careful, because around us prowling the "dream stealers".

Unfortunately always find obstacles to the realization of those dreams, things are not always easy but sometimes more difficult than material obstacles are the people around us, telling us:

- You can not.

- It's very difficult.

- Do not waste your time on this nonsense.

- It is very expensive is not for you.

- Better look for a job.

When we hear these phrases from people who do not care about we do not care, but when we hear from people close to us, really affect us and fill us with dismay, sadness, guilt and fear, fear of failure and recognize that they were right and they were right and we are wrong, these are our dreamthieves or so-called steals dreams and can be:

Our friends, family, neighbors, colleagues, can in be everywhere and not do so maliciously (although some do) most of the time trying to protect the bitter failure, avoid us wasting our time money and effort, and they do not want, but we undermine mind with phrases and negative comments.

Others on the contrary only reflected in their comments their own fears, frustrations and weaknesses and an unconscious or conscious way sometimes do not want anyone else to succeed just because they failed and are resentful.

These people are very numerous and fear "Your success" if your you manage to climb the mountain, they should also raise it, or acknowledge they were wrong, and you know, there is something that costs more, to admit defeat in your pride.

There are other dreams steals and this is more subtle, not seek to discourage you but you encourage but actually you induce to error to rip you off or scam you or taking advantage of you, after a bitter experience like this most people give up their dreams.

These are the bad advise you on purpose, that what they really want is your failure, and so get them wrong to remain kings guidelines. These people are dangerous to your side and you have them away from your life as soon as possible.

And best for last: ourselves! Yes, we have many times had dreams but ultimately we ourselves who we say this very difficult, I'm tired, I have no time, better tomorrow, and I have to do it every day !? and you have to invest something for free ?, no ?, is not for me, I can not afford it, etc. etc.

This situation is very common, as autodesmoralizamos ourselves for fear we succeed.

A dream is just the beginning of something, you decide whether it is more or ends before you start. A dream is like stand in front of a ladder and climb the first step, for others you need a plan, real determination, intelligence, perseverance, perseverance, hunger for victory, courage, passion, faith and even more. That's when a dream becomes a goal and have a much better chance of doing ..

Perhaps one of the hardest things a dream is to take action, it will always be easy to sit back, watch the stars and only dream, not bad to start but we must take action, very nice and good the dream but takes action never to materialize.

Decided to undertake, to make things clear that first we must investigate, think, study, seek advice itself but of people who have succeeded, share our dreams with people who are objective and support us and to share them, believing in us same, it may not always triumph to the first but we can always learn and improve over and over again until you do and feel that exquisite and deep satisfaction of success, accomplishment and achievement.

Remember the great changes, great discoveries, the great inventions began with a dream, some brothers dreamed that man could fly, a man dreamed that he had more land overseas and that the earth was round, a man dreamed that anyone could have a car when they were only for the rich, the world has been full of dreams became realities goals and then.

Everyone has happened to us that for some reason or circumstance of life we have abandoned our dreams, sometimes we allowed ourselves to be stolen, sometimes we have not defended as we should, sometimes we do not work enough on them, no matter what you have past is never too late to take them up again, to continue with our goals, life is not to see through a glass case, it is to go out and fight for the things that are important to us no matter what anyone else says that more important than that's what we tell ourselves.

Do not give up your dreams, your life better guide to them, may initially things are not very clear but if you persist with determination not as magically but things will become clearer.

Someone once told me, Embark, fight, and if you fail, get up and take back and fight, because only then you will get success, not ceasing to undertake and try to get your dreams.

As in the film Rocky 6;

I'll tell you something you already know, the world is not all joy and color. The world is a terrible place and how hard you are able to kneel shock and keep you permanently subject if you do not you prevent it. Neither you nor I nor anyone hits harder than life, but no matter how hard you hit but how hard you can hit. And you hold it as you go. Have to endure still advancing, this is how you win. If you know what you're worth go get what you deserve, but you'll have to endure the blows. And you can not be saying you're not where you wanted to get because of him, her or anybody, that they do cowards and you're not. You're capable of anything.

15. 10 keys to detect toxic people

Finally I'll tell you something that will help you on your journey through the murky waters of being an entrepreneur; to be a leader of Network Marketing.

Today you can devote to many professions occupationally. But few are as accessible and provide as many benefits as does the Network Marketing industry. If you want a profession that success will translate into more free time and quality to enjoy friends and family, you are in the right industry.

However, it requires an effort. As the Americans say: "No Pain, No Gain", and here is exactly that. You have to pay the price to get to the top in the industry of Network Marketing. That price you have to pay is the personal development that you have to submit. It seems incredible but your network marketing business grows to the level that you grow as a person. And some people do not want to go through this development, because their environment will look like a freak, either because it is comfortable or perhaps because it is not the time, because leaving the business. Because we are so capricious, just accusing the industry does not work in

Instead of assuming that we who did not do everything possible to make it work.

You have to understand that it takes 5-7 years to achieve financial freedom of media. Some arrive earlier and others arrive later. Many never get it. I do not know if you are willing to develop yourself, but you have two ways to do it. You can learn by experience, but this will take years or you can learn from those who have been there, and you have the secrets and tricks to arrive before bypassing the mistakes they made. To learn more about my personal history:www.juancarlosmartin.info/quien-soy/

So I wrote 10 Reasons to Avoid toxic people, because in Network Marketing or avoiding or your business will not grow. I'll give you an example: if you're a waiter, with all due respect to those who perform this type of work; you can charge money being surrounded by negative people because you go and do what your boss tells you your time running out and cobras, but Network Marketing is different. Going a step further, and you can not stand the change you require as a person being surrounded by a toxic environment. You will see how you grow and people around you stay in the same place they were one year ago.

There are many kinds of toxic person. For example: Some of them are jealous, childish, paranoid or selfish. There are many toxic personalities in society but all agree on one thing;

do nothing positive for a relationship, friendship, work, sentimental or even familiar. Destroy any attempt to create healthy and minimally cordial ties. When you are with a toxic person there is always bad rolls bother you absorb quickly and even psychically because you need only to them, do not stop asking and mainly manipulate you.

1   Reason
Your toxic friendships are very good psychologically, I guess your fears to know how to seduce you. First make us believe that, with your help, everything is possible, then have the power to manipulate at will. Able to adapt their behavior, but also its principles and values, based on the prototype of its victims.

2   Reason
They are skilled at turning around a situation, to present themselves as victims when in fact they are executioners. This is a false victimization, in order to seduce their prey and clear the ground for use others when needed.

Reason   3
Through partial lies distort reality and play two ways, as if they control the speech control thought. Become mixed with flattery insults in the same sentence hardly flinching.

Reason   4
They do not usually have ethical and moral principles. These vary depending on your goals or

context and others try to stay away from their particular set of values.

5   Reason
They look like predators, they are vampires who do not respect the autonomy of others and impose their own criteria. If when you're with them, you feel tired mentally, then you should take note because it is an alarm that you're being poisoned by your environment.

6   Reason
If you look closely, they are impervious to guilt always have us making us feel bad.

Reason   7
Usually excellent strategists, patient and constant until they reach their goal, but instead are uncreative.

Reason   8
Normally they sow doubt about the qualities and skills of others to discredit them and eliminate their self-esteem.

Reason   9
There are no moral taboos for toxic people, since others do not conceive as a person worthy of respect, but only as a more or less useful object.

last   Reason
They have an inconsistency between his speech and behavior; on the one hand mouth is filled with

altruistic proposals, while only then act based on their personal interest.

Conclusion:
Worst of all is that rob us of energy without us even noticing. And they are experts in relationships and engage hyperabsorbent art teachers intoxicate. It is not easy to identify at first sight and often do not realize which are toxic people until we found that after being with them always the same recurring negative feelings: exhaustion, frustration, stress or relief at being alone.

Often it is our own fault for denying deceive ourselves that we are surrounded by toxic people, "emotional vampires" because it is our best friend, partner or relative. Thoughts like "It will be my business" or "may be my fault" are thoughts that do nothing but prolong an unhealthy relationship.

It is true that we live in an environment conducive to the spread of toxic personalities such social context. A wave of neomaquiavelismo to which we must put a stop to win the appreciation and respect of whom around us.

FINISH !!!!!!!!

I hope you enjoyed reading this book. For me, it has been a pleasure and an honor to accompany you on this beautiful journey, which I hope I could help you better understand how to get to earn money through this industry that is selling network or sale Multilevel.

It is time to wish that you get the best hit you can get to get in life.

NEVER BE ABLE TO LIVE WITH AUTHENTIC passion, if you settle LIFE LESS THAN LIFE LIVED Pudistes HABER.

On the next page you have a great gift dear reader, if you think you can help with the development of your business wear it.

It's something you can not miss it for the world, ADVANTAGE.

A NOTE TO READERS

If the content of this book has proved interesting and useful for your business development and training of your team, please let me know.

If you have any anecdote, case study or any suggestions you'd like to share with others through my blog or my next book, please let me know too.

If you really liked this book and you want to share a project with me, I propose one thing, send me a photo where you show up with my book, along with a small testimony of what has brought you this book and enter your website and in the next publication of my blog will talk about you and your project.

Thank you thank you thank you.

I look forward to your stories, suggestions and opinions. You can contact me through my email info@juancarlosmartin.info or my blog www.juancarlosmartin.info/blog

Contact the author:

www.juancarlosmartin.info/

www.facebook.com/juancarlosmartinmm

www.facebook.com/consultorjuancarlosmmm/

https://twitter.com/CarlosExialoe

www.linkedin.com/in/consultorjuancarlosmmm/

www.instagram.com/juancarlosmartinmm/

MY GIFT ...

Dear reader, here I leave my most precious gift, made me expand my network in a very short tiempo.Descargatelo is in PDF format.

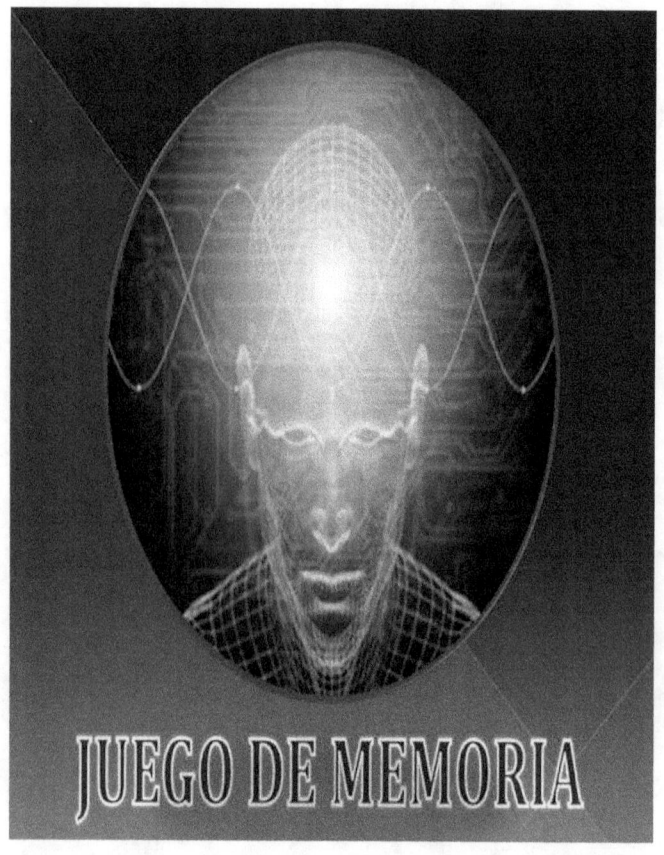

You only have to enter:
www.juancarlosmartin.info/juegodememoria

YOU'VE GOT NOTHING TO LOSE

And much to gain

SEE YOU ON THE ROAD TO SUCCESS

READER SERVICE

+34 685 24 73 45

info@juancarlosmartin.info

www.ingramcontent.com/pod-product-compliance
Lightning Source LLC
Chambersburg PA
CBHW060840170526
45158CB00001B/197